Searchlight
BOOKS™

Getting into Government

Exploring

Media and Government

Jennifer Joline Anderson

Lerner Publications ◆ Minneapolis

Lerner Publications Company
An imprint of Lerner Publishing Group, Inc.
241 First Avenue North
Minneapolis, MN 55401 USA

For reading levels and more information, look up this title
at www.lernerbooks.com.

Library of Congress Cataloging-in-Publication Data

Names: Anderson, Jennifer Joline, author.
Title: Exploring media and government / Jennifer Joline Anderson.
Description: Minneapolis : Lerner Publications, 2020. | Series: Searchlight books. Getting into government | Includes bibliographical references and index. | Audience: Age 8–11. | Audience: Grade 4 to 6.
Identifiers: LCCN 2018057823 (print) | LCCN 2018061001 (ebook) | ISBN 9781541556768 (eb pdf) | ISBN 9781541555860 (lb : alk. paper) | ISBN 9781541574779 (pb : alk. paper)
Subjects: LCSH: Press and politics—United States—Juvenile literature. | Mass media—Political aspects—United States—Juvenile literature. | Government and the press—United States—Juvenile literature. | Freedom of the press—United States—Juvenile literature.
Classification: LCC P95.82.U6 (ebook) | LCC P95.82.U6 A535 2020 (print) | DDC 071/.3—dc23

LC record available at https://lccn.loc.gov/2018057823

Manufactured in the United States of America
1-46041-43364-3/11/2019

Contents

Chapter 1

WHAT IS THE MEDIA?

The president is holding a press conference at the White House. The room is filled with reporters. Bright lights and video cameras point at the president, who stands in front of a microphone. Everyone waits to hear what the president has to say. When the speech is over, they will have questions to ask.

Presidents hold press conferences to share important information with large audiences.

TV news reporters tell the public what the president said in a press conference.

When the president of the United States speaks, it becomes news around the world. The press conference will be shared on TV, radio, and the internet. Newspapers and magazines will report it in many different languages. People will discuss what the president said. They may share their opinions about the job the president is doing.

Newspapers and magazines often contain more in-depth stories than television and radio. They sometimes contain opinion pieces as well.

Forms of Media

News about the government is shared through the media. The media includes many forms of communication that can reach large numbers of people. Television, radio, the internet, and print newspapers and magazines are all forms of media.

People who report the news in the media are called the press. Reporters, photographers, radio and TV announcers, and other members of the press work hard to share the news. These days, news can be shared more quickly and easily than ever before.

Members of the press surround a politician to get information for the news stories they will write.

Chapter 2

FREEDOM OF THE PRESS

On Election Day, citizens vote to select new leaders.

The United States is a democracy. That means the citizens choose their leaders by voting in elections. People are free to use the press, or the media, to share information and opinions about the government. This right is called freedom of the press.

Keeping People Informed

The media is important for democracy. It gives people information so they can decide how to vote. Before an election, people can read the newspaper to learn about the candidates. Candidates may go on television to participate in debates. During a debate, candidates answer questions about what they will do if elected.

Candidates running for office often discuss issues in a debate. This helps citizens decide who to vote for.

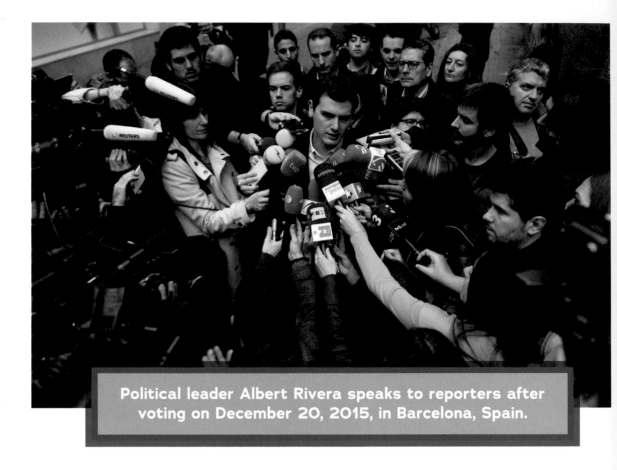

Political leader Albert Rivera speaks to reporters after voting on December 20, 2015, in Barcelona, Spain.

Reporters gather the news. Their job is to give the facts. To uncover the truth, they act like detectives. When a politician says something, it is the reporter's job to check whether that statement is true. Reporters ask tough questions and investigate by interviewing different sources. This helps make sure politicians are being honest and doing their job well.

That's a Fact!

The press is powerful. It can even stop a president who is breaking the law. In 1972, people working for President Richard Nixon were caught stealing information from an office building called Watergate. The president knew about the burglary, but he lied about what he knew. Reporters worked hard to learn the truth. They published the story in the *Washington Post* newspaper. Many people who read the Watergate story were angry. In 1974, Nixon resigned from office and left the White House.

When Nixon resigned, it made headlines in newspapers.

Sharing Opinions and Ideas

Our freedoms allow people to share their opinions and ideas with others in the community. People can write letters to the editor of a magazine or newspaper. They can call in to a radio talk show. They can make comments on social media.

JUNE 17, 2015 | SHARE

LETTER TO THE EDITOR: NY TIMES

The New York Times

DNA and the F.B.I.

MAY 5, 2015

To the Editor:

As "Junk Science at the F.B.I." (editorial, April 27) noted, the fact that microscopic hair examiners at the agency gave erroneous testimony in 96 percent of the cases reviewed so far could result in more exonerations for crimes the convicted didn't commit.

This is a pretty safe bet when you consider that faulty microscopic hair analysis was a contributing factor in 22 percent of the 329 DNA exonerations nationwide.

A LETTER TO THE EDITOR FROM THE *NEW YORK TIMES*

Politicians also use the media. Many politicians have accounts on Facebook and Twitter. People have a chance to hear what these leaders think. But politicians do not control what other people say about them in the media.

Freedom of the press is a right of all Americans.

Censorship and the Media

In some countries, the government controls what people can say or print in the media. This is called censorship. In the United States, the government allows people freedom of speech and freedom of the press. The government will not censor information unless it is top secret or could cause danger to citizens. That means people are free to speak out and share their ideas. The media gives people a voice in their government.

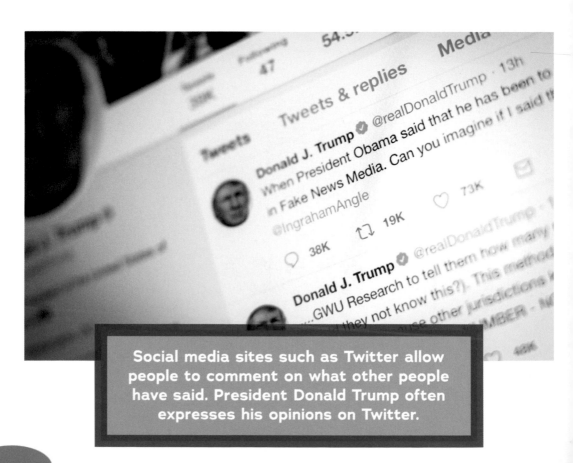

Social media sites such as Twitter allow people to comment on what other people have said. President Donald Trump often expresses his opinions on Twitter.

Government Affects You

Freedom of speech and freedom of the press are rights that apply to you. You can share your opinions about the government with your friends. You can make signs for a political cause you believe in. Young people have gotten together and talked to the media to make changes in their own communities.

In the United States, people of all ages have the right to speak up for their beliefs.

Chapter 3

CAN WE TRUST THE MEDIA?

During an election year, the media is full of news stories, opinion articles, and political ads. Every day the news features stories about the candidates. You see political ads frequently when you watch television. People argue about one side or the other. Who is right? Can we really trust the media?

STATE OF THE UNION

TV news journalists and other members of the press report on big events, such as the president's State of the Union address.

It's a journalist's responsibility to carefully research the articles that he or she writes.

Fact or Opinion?

Members of the news media are supposed to report facts. These facts must be correct. Major newspapers, TV networks, and radio stations hire fact-checkers. Their job is to make sure all the facts are correct before a story is shared.

The media also shares opinions about government. Opinions are what people think or feel. Newspapers have opinion articles. People with different opinions discuss issues on television and radio talk shows. Opinions are also shared on the internet. People should not trust every opinion they hear. Instead, they should listen carefully to many points of view before deciding whom they agree with the most.

Talk shows such as *Face the Nation* allow reporters and experts to discuss political matters and give their opinions.

US POLITICS LIVE

US ELECTIONS 2016

2016 PRESIDENTIAL ELECTIONS   POLICY AND REGULATION   BUSINESS AND ECONOMY

BREAKING NEWS: PRESIDENT OBAMA CONFIRMS HE WILL REFUSE TO LEAVE OFFICE IF TRUMP IS ELECTED

BREAKING NEWS
OBAMA:"I WON'T LEAVE IF TRUMP IS ELECTED" CNN

This fake story about President Barack Obama is made to look like a real story from Cable News Network (CNN), but it is not really from CNN.

Fake News

Fake news stories are made up and do not come from trustworthy sources. Sometimes they are on the internet, in tabloid magazines, or on entertainment news shows. Some fake stories are written as jokes. Others are made up to do harm. Fake stories may include real photos and details to trick people into believing the story is true. Fake news stories often spread when people who believe the stories share them on social media.

That's a Fact!

During the 2016 election year, fake news articles appeared on Facebook. One story said Hillary Clinton had a terrible disease. There were fake stories about Donald Trump too. These stories tricked many people. The fake stories might have changed how people voted. After the election, Facebook began working harder to weed out fake news stories and keep them from spreading on the social media site.

This fake news story says Hillary Clinton sold weapons to enemies.

PEOPLE RUNNING FOR OFFICE USE POSITIVE POLITICAL ADS TO MAKE PEOPLE WANT TO VOTE FOR THEM.

Political Ads

During an election year, you may see political ads on TV or hear them on the radio. Political ads cannot be trusted as fact. They are made to convince people to support one candidate instead of another.

ROMNEY'S NOT
THE SOLUTION.
HE'S THE PROBLEM.

APPROVED BY BARACK OBAMA. PAID FOR BY OBAMA FOR AMERICA

Negative ads try to make a candidate look bad so that voters will vote against him or her.

Positive ads make a candidate look good. They include messages to make the candidate look strong and likeable. Negative ads make another candidate look bad. These ads might stretch the truth or use name-calling or other negative words to attack a candidate.

Government Affects You

Negative ads on TV can be upsetting to some viewers. These ads sometimes use scary music and say bad things about a candidate. Remember that a political ad is just like any other commercial. Commercials are made to get people to buy things, such as a new toy or a breakfast cereal. Political ads are made to get people to vote for a candidate. You should not believe everything an ad says. If you see an ad that scares or worries you, ask an adult to help you figure out what the ad really means.

Some ads and images on TV can seem unsettling. Talk with an adult if you see something that worries you on TV or online.

After a press conference in China in 2005, President George W. Bush tried to leave through a locked door. The media focused more on his mistake than why he was in China in the first place—to meet with the country's president.

What's the Whole Story?

Sometimes the media tells only part of the story. For instance, a politician may give a long interview. The TV station might not have time for the whole interview. Only part of what the politician said will be on TV. This is called a sound bite. If a politician slipped up and said something silly, the media may report the mistake. The media might ignore the rest of what the politician said.

The media sometimes focuses on things that are not very important. For example, a reporter may comment on a political candidate's hair, clothing, or personal life rather than talking about what the candidate plans to do if elected. Such stories may be entertaining to some, but they don't provide information about where the candidate stands on important issues.

When Hillary Clinton was running for president, the news media spent a lot of time reporting on her hair and clothing.

Chapter 4

THE MEDIA AND YOU

News about political figures and the government is everywhere. You can watch the news on television or hear it on the radio. You can read newspapers and magazines in print or on the internet. Some news is especially for kids. Your teacher may share a news magazine with you at school.

Find a news magazine designed especially for kids or read the newspaper with a parent or teacher. Ask him or her to explain things you do not understand.

During an election year, the TV news is buzzing with information. Watch a news show with an adult, and listen to what the reporters say. See if you can tell which statements are facts and which are just someone's opinion. If you see a political ad, ask yourself what the ad wants you to believe.

You can learn a lot by watching the news and political talk shows. If you need help figuring out what are facts and what are opinions, ask a trusted adult.

How can you tell if a story is real or just fake news? Before you believe the headlines, think about where the news is coming from. Is it from a news network, magazine, or newspaper you've heard of before? If not, it could be fake news. Try to find another source for the story. If in doubt, ask a teacher, librarian, or another adult to help you.

Freedom of the press means that not everything that gets reported is necessarily true. Be a detective and see if you can tell fact from fiction in the news.

Who's Right?

Many people like to get their news from social media, such as Facebook and Twitter. There, they can share news articles with friends. They can also post videos or make comments. Social media lets people consider many points of view.

Others warn that social media is not trustworthy. People may share fake news. They may share opinions that don't make sense. People may share articles that are funny or silly. They may ignore important news.

What do you think? When you get older, will you choose to get your news on social media? Why or why not?

Glossary

candidate: a person who is running in an election

censorship: removing parts of a book, movie, or other work or controlling what people share in the media

debate: a discussion in which people express different opinions

fact-checker: a person who checks the facts in a news story

investigate: to gather information about something

opinion: your personal feelings about someone or something

politician: a person who runs for or holds a government office, such as a senator

press conference: a meeting in which someone gives information to news reporters and answers questions

resign: to give up a job, position, or office voluntarily

social media: websites and apps that allow people to connect with others and share information

tabloid: a newspaper or magazine that contains stories about famous people and other less serious news items that aren't necessarily true

Learn More about Media and Government

Books

Braun, Eric. *Taking Action for Civil and Political Rights.* Minneapolis: Lerner Publications, 2017. Kids around the world use the media to make a difference. Read this book to learn more about how you can take action too.

Harris, Duchess. *The Fake News Phenomenon.* Minneapolis: Core Library, 2018. How can you tell if something you read is fake news? Read this title to learn about how to make good choices when using the media.

Mara, Wil. *Politics and the Media.* Ann Arbor, MI: Cherry Lake Publishing, 2019. For hundreds of years, the media has played a role in shaping political decisions. This book takes a historical look at the relationship between politics and the media.

Websites

KidsPost
https://www.washingtonpost.com/lifestyle/kidspost
The *Washington Post* newspaper publishes some news just for kids. Check it out at this website.

PBS Kids Speak Out
https://pbskids.org/speakout/
Kids can share their opinions about government in the media.
Visit this website to see what kids are saying and share your own ideas too.

Index

Photo Acknowledgments

Image credits: Mark Wilson/Getty Images, p. 4; Chip Somodevilla/Getty Images, p. 5; Yongyuan Dai/Getty Images, p. 6; Ethan Miller/Getty Images, p. 7; Jay LaPrete/Getty Images, p. 8; Win McNamee/Getty Images, p. 9; David Ramos/Getty Images, p. 10; Bettmann/Getty Images, p. 11; accessed via Google, pp. 12, 19, 22; Jauhien Krajko/500px/Getty Images, p. 13; Jaap Arriens/NurPhoto/Getty Images, p. 14; Diego G Diaz/Shutterstock.com, p. 15; Mary Kouw/CBS/Getty Images, p. 16; dennizn/Shutterstock.com, p. 17; Chris Usher/CBS/Getty Images, p. 18; The Photo Works/Alamy Stock Photo, p. 20; AP Photo/Jae C. Hong, p. 21; J Walters/Shutterstock.com, p. 23; PAUL J. RICHARDS/AFP/Getty Images, p. 24; Justin Sullivan/Getty Images, p. 25; George Rudy/Shutterstock.com, p. 26; Stígur Már Karlsson/Heimsmyndir/Getty Images, p. 27; Amer Ghazzal/Barcroft Images/Getty Images, p. 28; aradaphotography/Shutterstock.com, p. 29.

Cover: Mandel Ngan/AFP/Getty Images.

Main body text set in Adrianna Regular 14/20.
Typeface provided by Chank.